Serve with a Heart Like Jesus

*Scriptures, Reflections and
Encouragement for All Who Serve*

Written by Bart Tesoriero

All Scripture quotations, unless otherwise indicated, are taken from the Holy Bible, New International Version®, NIV®. Copyright ©1973, 1978, 1984, 2011 by Biblica, Inc.™ Used by permission of Zondervan. All rights reserved worldwide. www.zondervan.com The "NIV" and "New International Version" are trademarks registered in the United States Patent and Trademark Office by Biblica, Inc.™

Scripture quotations designated NRSV are taken from the New Revised Standard Version Bible, copyright 1989, Division of Christian Education of the National Council of the Churches of Christ in the United States of America. Used by permission. All rights reserved.

Scripture quotations marked (TLB) are taken from The Living Bible copyright © 1971. Used by permission of Tyndale House Publishers, Inc., Carol Stream, Illinois 60188. All rights reserved.

ISBN 978-1-61796-284-4
Artwork and Text © 2018, Living Grace

To

_____

From

_____

Date

_____

The Christian who is pure and without fault, from God the Father's point of view, is the one who takes care of orphans and widows, and who remains true to the Lord—not soiled and dirtied by his contacts with the world.

–James 1:27 (TLB)

"Whoever wants to become great among you must be your servant ... just as the Son of Man did not come to be served, but to serve, and to give his life as a ransom for many."

–Matthew 20:26, 28

His Heart

It is an honor to serve with the heart of Jesus. He is the only-begotten Son of the Eternal Father, through whom the whole universe was created. He is the Alpha and the Omega; the Beginning and the End. He is the second Person of the Blessed Trinity, and with the Father and the Holy Spirit dwells in unapproachable light and splendor.

At the same time, Jesus is Emmanuel, God with us. Paul writes to the Philippians that Jesus, "being in very nature God, did not consider equality with God something to be used to his own advantage; rather, he made himself nothing by taking the very nature of a servant, being made in human likeness. And being found in appearance as a man, he humbled himself by becoming obedient to death— even death on a cross!" (Philippians 2:6-8).

So we see that although he could have "lorded" it over everyone and would have been entirely within his rights to do so, Jesus instead came among us a servant. In doing so, he revealed the true nature of the Father's heart—it is the heart of one who came not to be served but to serve, the heart of a Father who runs to embrace his prodigal children, the heart of a good shepherd who lays down his life for his sheep.

Your Heart

This is the God who is inviting you to serve. The first thing to know is that He loves you. Your heart matters to God! He has come to serve you.

This is love: not that we loved God, but that he loved us and sent his Son as an atoning sacrifice for our sins.

–1 John 4:10

Does that sound preposterous? Consider this. There is an old Latin proverb: *Nemo dat quod non habet.* Roughly translated it means, "You can't give what you haven't got!"

You and I can best serve others if we first realize that our Father is embracing us with his love, that we are accepted in the Beloved. We can serve others if we first take time to realize that out of his endless mercy, Jesus has freely given the atonement for our sins and for the sins of the whole world. We can receive that love, look the world in the eye, and stand free.

You, my brothers and sisters, were called to be free. But do not use your freedom to indulge the flesh; rather, serve one another humbly in love.

–Galatians 5:13

Whoever serves me must follow me; and where I am, my servant also will be. My Father will honor the one who serves me.

–John 12:26

It is a blessing to serve the Lord. When you think about it, really, to serve as Jesus served is to allow Jesus to serve in you. What would that look like to you? Or better said, how do you appear to others when you allow Jesus to serve through you?

_____

_____

_____

_____

You did not choose me, but I chose you and appointed you so that you might go and bear fruit–fruit that will last.

–John 15:16

It is a great honor to serve the Lord. It is a special blessing to serve him by serving his people. But the truth is, we cannot even do that unless he calls us.

Then I heard the voice of the Lord saying, "Whom shall I send? And who will go for us?" And I said, "Here am I. Send me!"

–Isaiah 6:8

After we receive God's deep and personal love for us, after being born from above through water and the Holy Spirit, after surrendering to God's love, we need to listen for his call. How does God call us?

Father, help me know my true identity and what truly matters. Help me to feel your deep and true love for me in my heart. Please help me to quiet down, to be still and know, and to listen for your voice speaking to my heart. What is your call for me? Where and how can I let your light shine out through me? How can I be Christ to others this day?

_____

_____

_____

Thank you Father. In Jesus' name. Amen.

You Can't Steer a Parked Car

Once you've listened to God and have some sense of his direction, it's time to move.

Serving as a Christian means playing ON and FOR Jesus' team. Fans may wear jerseys and sit in the stands, but they aren't on the team or in the game. If the first disciples had simply been fans of Jesus, the cheering would have stopped when Jesus "left the field" and you and I wouldn't know, love, or live for Jesus today. You may not be called or gifted to be an evangelist or preacher, but you do have a calling and purpose from God—his work for you to accomplish. Discovering and living out your purpose is rewarding, humbling, challenging, often amazing, and yes, God's goodness for you.

Now you are the body of Christ, and each one of you is a part of it. And God has placed in the church first of all apostles, second prophets, third teachers, then miracles, then gifts of healing, of helping, of guidance, and of different kinds of tongues. Are all apostles? Are all prophets? Are all teachers? Do all work miracles? Do all have gifts of healing? Do all speak in tongues? Do all interpret? Now eagerly desire the greater gifts.
–1 Corinthians 12:27-31

Prayers for a Servant Heart

Prayer of Saint Francis of Assisi

Lord,

Make me an instrument of Thy peace.

Where there is hatred, let me sow love.

Where there is injury, pardon;

Where there is doubt, faith;

Where there is despair, hope;

Where there is darkness, light;

And where there is sadness, joy.

O Divine Master, grant that I may not so much seek

To be consoled, as to console;

To be understood, as to understand;

To be loved, as to love;

For it is in giving that we receive;

It is in pardoning that we are pardoned;

And it is in dying that we are born to eternal life.

Amen.

If you enjoy organizing, giving, accounting, hospitality, coaching, helping with health care, answering phones, praying, arts and crafts, fixing IT problems, caring for kids, or serving others in any way, you ARE on the team and in the game. Just ask; God WILL give you desires from his heart, and courage to overcome your insecurity and fill you with purpose. If he was willing to give his son Jesus to die for you, he will put you in the game as well!

Dear God, I know you made me, and today I choose to believe you made me for purposes beyond my own self, needs, and fears. I'm willing to be willing, so please put YOUR desires in my heart, and help me to fulfill your purposes for me. I do enjoy _____, so for starters, please show me how you might be calling me to _____ for YOUR glory and desires. Amen.

Yet you, LORD, are our Father. We are the clay, you are the potter; we are all the work of your hand.

–Isaiah 64:8

Let God Shape You

Pottery making was a necessary and well-known trade in Bible times. The Lord spoke to his people with this imagery especially through the prophets Isaiah and Jeremiah. The apostle Paul also uses this metaphor in his letter to the Romans.

Many of us today are less familiar with pottery making than those in Bible times, though we have some idea of how it's done. We know that potters have workshops and potter's wheels, upon which they turn their pottery, fashioning the clay as it spins before them.

The Lord said something rather interesting to the prophet Jeremiah:

> This is the word that came to Jeremiah from the LORD: "Go down to the potter's house, and there I will give you my message." So I went down to the potter's house, and I saw him working at the wheel. But the pot he was shaping from the clay was marred in his hands; so the potter formed it into another pot, shaping it as seemed best to him.

Then the word of the LORD came to me. He said, "Can I not do with you, Israel, as this potter does?" declares the LORD. "Like clay in the hand of the potter, so are you in my hand, Israel. If at any time I announce that a nation or kingdom is to be uprooted, torn down and destroyed, and if that nation I warned repents of its evil, then I will relent and not inflict on it the disaster I had planned. And if at another time I announce that a nation or kingdom is to be built up and planted, and if it does evil in my sight and does not obey me, then I will reconsider the good I had intended to do for it."

–Jeremiah 18:1-10

It's pretty clear that God is the Master, and we are the clay. That being said, we are not inert. Each one of us has a free will, and we can either allow God to shape us or we can resist. God calls us to cooperate with him. So, unlike a potter who works with a passive lump of clay, God works with us in our imaginations, hearts, and wills to create something of beauty for his Kingdom. Are you willing to let God have his way in you today?

The Glory of God is man fully alive!
–Saint Irenaeus, an early Father of the Church

Prayer To Let God Shape Me

Dear Heavenly Father, you have known all my days before I was conceived in my mother's womb. Help me, Lord, to hear your voice in my heart, to discern your plan—the divine design that you have chosen for me, and to follow. O dear God, I want to be in the center of your will and in the center of your heart. Help me to not follow the empty desires of my heart, but rather to seek to serve as your Son Jesus did. I choose to surrender to you and to allow you to shape me as you please. Please live your life through me, dear God. For then I will be truly happy and I will be a blessing to others. And for that, I thank you. Amen.

Trusting in God as He Molds Us

It is a wonderful thing to allow God into your heart. To know that the Father loves you is truly a deep and rich experience. Jesus experienced this in his own life here on earth. Do you remember the account of his baptism in the Jordan?

> As soon as Jesus was baptized, he went up out of the water. At that moment heaven was opened, and he saw the Spirit of God descending like a dove and alighting on him. And a voice from heaven said, "This is my Son, whom I love; with him I am well pleased."
>
> –Matthew 3:16-17

Jesus knew that the Father was very fond of him, and we can know this too, for each person who has received Jesus, who is born again from above, has a new life living in their heart. Paul teaches us this clearly: "Therefore, if anyone is in Christ, the new creation has come: The old has gone, the new is here!" (2 Corinthians 5:17).

This new life is a life of dependence on God, as a child depends on her father and mother, to give her what she needs. This does not mean that we sit back and just wait for God to do something, but rather that we rise each day and offer ourselves and our lives to God, and ask Him to come and live through us, through the gifts and talents and abilities He's given us, to serve Him and others. This new life means we decide to trust God each morning for what he has planned for us, and to follow his leading and nudges throughout the day.

It is not how much you do,
but how much love you put in the doing.
  –Mother Teresa

Love seeks one thing only: the good of the one loved.
Love is its own reward.
  –Thomas Merton

The closest thing to being cared for
is to care for someone else.
  –Carson McCullers

Caring about others, running the risk of feeling, and leaving an
impact on people brings happiness.
  –Rabbi Harold Kushner

Serving in the Family

At the World Meeting of Families in Philadelphia a few years ago, Pope Francis declared that mercy is first experienced in our families. He shared that, "like happiness, holiness is always tied to little gestures." Reminding us of Jesus' promise that those who give even a cup of water in His name would be rewarded, the pope said, "These little gestures are those we learn at home, in the family; they get lost amid all the other things we do, yet they do make each day different."

Pope Francis asserted that among these little gestures are "the quiet things done by mothers and grandmothers, by fathers and grandfathers, by children." He said these are "little signs of tenderness, affection and compassion." He cited other examples of tender love: "the warm supper we look forward to at night, the early lunch awaiting someone who gets up early to go to work." He added that these gestures could include "a blessing before we go to bed, or a hug after we return from a hard day's work."

God invites us to live mercy in our families. "Jesus tells us not to hold back these little miracles," says the pope. "Instead, he wants us to encourage them, to spread them. He asks us to go through life, our everyday life, encouraging all these little signs of love as signs of his own living and active presence in our world."

The Final Judgment

"When the Son of Man comes in his glory, and all the angels with him, he will sit on his glorious throne. All the nations will be gathered before him, and he will separate the people one from another as a shepherd separates the sheep from the goats. He will put the sheep on his right and the goats on his left.

"Then the King will say to those on his right, 'Come, you who are blessed by my Father; take your inheritance, the kingdom prepared for you since the creation of the world. For I was hungry and you gave me something to eat, I was thirsty and you gave me something to drink, I was a stranger and you invited me in, I needed clothes and you clothed me, I was sick and you looked after me, I was in prison and you came to visit me.'

"Then the righteous will answer him, 'Lord, when did we see you hungry and feed you, or thirsty and give you something to drink? When did we see you a stranger and invite you in, or needing clothes and clothe you? When did we see you sick or in prison and go to visit you?'

'The King will reply, 'Truly I tell you, whatever you did for one of the least of these brothers and sisters of mine, you did for me.'

'Then he will say to those on his left, 'Depart from me, you who are cursed, into the eternal fire prepared for the devil and his angels. For I was hungry and you gave me nothing to eat, I was thirsty and you gave me nothing to drink, I was a stranger and you did not invite me in, I needed clothes and you did not clothe me, I was sick and in prison and you did not look after me.'

'They also will answer, 'Lord, when did we see you hungry or thirsty or a stranger or needing clothes or sick or in prison, and did not help you?'

'He will reply, 'Truly I tell you, whatever you did not do for one of the least of these, you did not do for me.'

'Then they will go away to eternal punishment, but the righteous to eternal life."

–Matthew 25:31-46

Reach Out and Touch

"I, John, your brother, who share with you the distress, the kingdom, and the endurance we have in Jesus."

–Revelation 1:9

Bill Watson, the co-founder of Alcoholics Anonymous, discovered an amazing way to sustain his own sobriety: help other alcoholics! While the general principle of serving others is certainly a hallmark of most religions, Bill W. and his friends learned from experience that working with other alcoholics was the single most powerful antidote to alcoholism. They therefore incorporated this directive into the 12th Step: "Carry this message to others!"

It is vitally important when serving, whether it's in a ministry or perhaps as a caregiver, to regularly meet with others in order to encourage and be encouraged. Our own inner spiritual health is the fruit of serving others and of following Jesus our Lord. God's power fuels our daily walk, which is typically experienced in community with others who share our weaknesses and our hope in Christ.

Each one of us can reach out and touch in our own unique way, and help as no one else can. As we watch those we serve heal and recover, and then often go on to help others themselves, we see their loneliness and apprehension give way to fellowship and assurance. When this happens, we ourselves are buoyed up and encouraged. Our souls are satisfied. We're on our way home!

Only a Spark

I am only a spark;

make me a fire.

I am only a string;

make me a lyre.

I am only a drop;

make me a fountain.

I am only an ant hill;

make me a mountain.

I am only a feather;

make me a wing.

I am only a rag;

make me a king.

O God, Use Me

They that hope in the LORD will renew their strength, they

will soar as with eagles' wings;

They will run and not grow weary,

walk and not grow faint.

–Isaiah 40:31

Dear Heavenly Father,

I just want to praise you today for you! You created me, you called me into being, you sent your dear Son Jesus to redeem me, and now you have chosen me to be yours forever. Thank you!

Dear God, you have a purpose for which you created me, and I humbly ask you to please help me fulfill it. I trust that you are going to walk ahead of me regardless of how the enemy may try to thwart your work. I claim your promise to your servant Joshua: "Have I not commanded you? Be strong and courageous. Do not be afraid; do not be discouraged, for the LORD your God will be with you wherever you go" (Joshua 1:9).

O Lord, you have commanded us to keep your precepts diligently. Help me to seek you early with all my heart, to spend time in your presence so that you can have your way in me. Use me as you see fit. I give myself to you. This I ask, dear Father, in the name of your beloved Son, Jesus. Amen.

*The best way to find yourself
is to lose yourself in the service of others.*
–Mahatma Gandhi

A Life of Service

From the time she was a small child, my friend's older sister knew she was called to be a nurse. As a teenager, she cared for her aging grandfather. Her younger sister looked up to her and decided she wanted to become a nurse as well. These two sisters have spent their entire adult lives helping heal the sick. They also guided their parents' journey into eternal life.

No matter what our calling is in life, we all need to serve others for in so doing we discover our common vocation: to love. When we take the focus off ourselves and reach out to help others, guess what? We find joy.

Life becomes harder for us when we live for others, but it also becomes richer and happier.
–Albert Schweitzer

Give, and it will be given to you. A good measure, pressed down, shaken together and running over, will be poured into your lap. For with the measure you use, it will be measured to you.
–Luke 6:38

The Road Less Traveled

Serving others is one way to take the focus off our own troubles, but if you want to experience real joy, throw your heart and soul into giving. There's a joy that comes when we give of ourselves to serve others on a regular basis, in spite of all the challenges. The world calls us to indulge ourselves; the Lord calls us to lives of generous service and self-forgetfulness. When we do that, he repays us a hundred fold.

Let us seek to follow Jesus' example of servant leadership. There are wonderful men, women, and children waiting to be met, to be served, to be loved. And who knows, we might even discover a short-cut to joy!

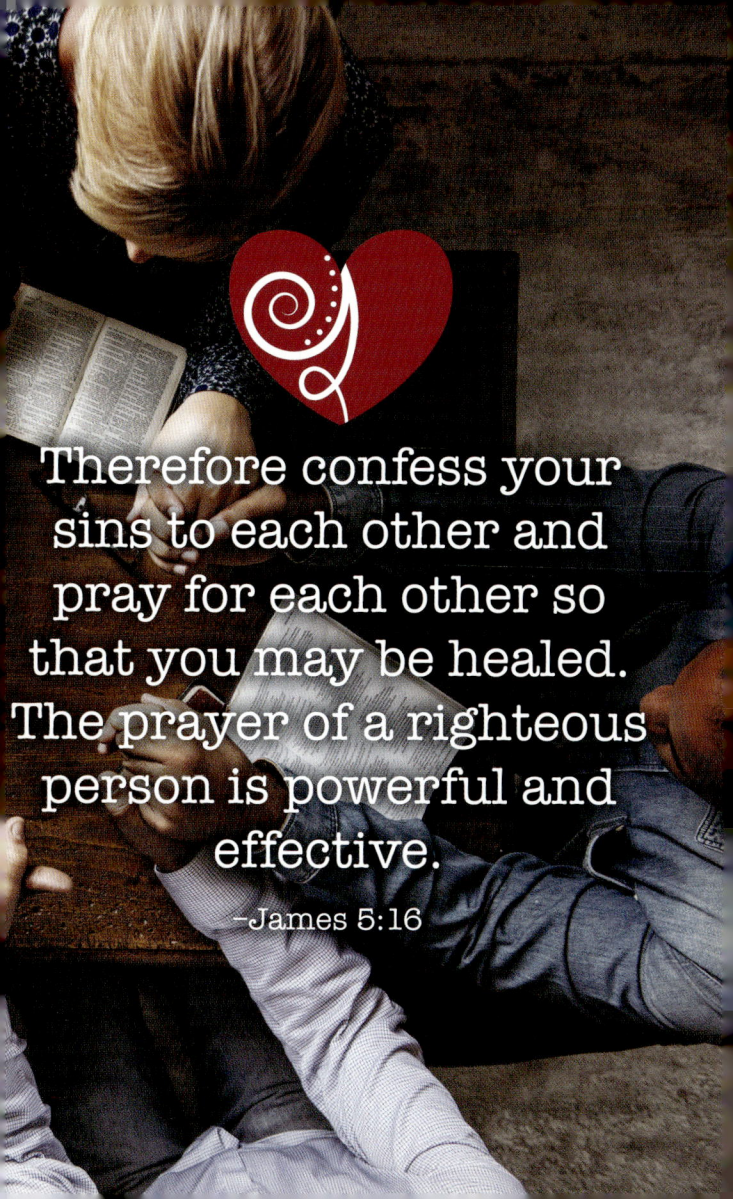

Spiritual Works of Mercy

Jesus calls us to serve by meeting both the physical and spiritual needs of others. Below are some examples of the latter.

Counsel the Doubtful

Be present to others when they speak to you, especially if they need to pour out their heart and share their burdens and difficulties. Ask the Holy Spirit to help you truly discern what they need before responding.

Speak the truth in love to a brother or sister who might be struggling, calling them to be faithful to the Lord and his Gospel. Make yourself available to those who could use your help. If possible, reach out to them and offer your encouragement and support.

Take time to study the truth, especially in the Scripture and other good books, so that you will be ready to help someone in need move from darkness to the light.

Instruct the Uninformed

Take a class or join a Bible study group to learn more about your faith. Invite others to join you, and share your understanding and experience, especially with those who may be open to the Lord or questioning.

Be willing to share your own gifts, skills, and knowledge with others in the areas in which they could benefit. Reach out and offer to help or "tutor" others who want to learn about Jesus and his Good News.

Read good books and either form a small discussion group or just encourage others to read as well. Volunteer to teach a class at your church, or offer your help wherever needed on a Retreat or Day of Renewal.

Speak the Truth

Not many people like to hear that they are sinning or acting unjustly, especially in our "politically correct" culture. That being said, we are called as Christians to speak the truth in love to our fellow believers, calling them to be faithful to the Lord and his Gospel.

Jesus instructs us: "If your brother or sister sins, go and point out their fault, just between the two of you. If they listen to you, you have won them over. But if they will not listen, take one or two others along, so that 'every matter may be established by the testimony of two or three witnesses.' If they still refuse to listen, tell it to the church; and if they refuse to listen even to the church, treat them as you would a pagan or a tax collector" (Matthew 18:15-17).

So, if you see someone dishonoring the Lord in some way, pray for the Holy Spirit to prepare their heart, and ask the Spirit of Jesus to give you the right words, the right time, and the right way to speak to them.

If people around you start gossiping about someone, walk away, ask them to stop, or change the subject. Likewise, step up and intervene if you see someone hurting themselves or another.

Comfort the Afflicted

How can you comfort someone in distress? Listen. People who are suffering often find a great relief in someone who listens compassionately to them as they share their pain and difficulties.

Be there for others. Visit them. Offer to help where needed. Consider cooking a dinner or bringing over some groceries when a family is suffering a misfortune. Call someone who is going through a difficult time. Encourage them. Offer to pray with those who are afflicted in any way.

Forgive Offenses

Vengeance is mine, I will repay, says the Lord.

–Romans 12:19

If someone tells you they are sorry for something or asks your forgiveness, then forgive them in a clear and sincere manner, e.g., "I forgive you." This may seem obvious, yet forgiveness needs to be freely given in order to be freely received.

If someone has wronged you in any way and has NOT asked your forgiveness, pray for the grace to forgive them and then do so. Remember that forgiveness frees you as well as the other. Call to mind also the Scripture: "Forgive us our sins, for we also forgive everyone who sins against us" (Luke 11:4).

Have the humility to ask others for their forgiveness as well. Surrender resentments to God and pray for anyone who has either intentionally or unintentionally offended you. Pray for the grace to love them with the love of Jesus.

Bear Wrongs Patiently

Love is patient, love is kind.

-1 Corinthians 13:4

God calls us to serve others by ignoring their character defects whenever possible. He calls us to be less critical of others, and to give them the benefit of the doubt. We are to look for the good in others. Ask for the grace to see Jesus in them.

Another way to serve is to pray for those who wrong you. (One option would be The Prayer of Saint Francis, on page 12.) Remember that change comes about in God's time, not ours. A final way to serve is to think twice before saying nothing.

Pray for Others

Daily bring the needs of the whole world to the Lord in prayer. Consider visiting those who are grieving and offering them your sympathy and support.

Over the ages, Christians have found these and other physical and spiritual works of mercy to be a practical way of living out Jesus' new commandment. God simply asks us to love. He does not ask us to take on these works of mercy as some sort of extra burden. Rather, he wants us to ask him to fill us first with his love, with the heart and compassion of Jesus for us. Let us ask God to remove anything impeding us from an encounter with him. Then, let us reach out and act to love others with his love. In this way, Jesus heals his children.

I have made you known to them, and will continue to make you known in order that the love you have for me may be in them and that I myself may be in them.

–John 17:26

God's Telescope

The light that shines furthest shines brightest at home.

-Charles Studd

It is good to serve, and we are created to care for our brothers and sisters. That being said, we are called to be prudent in our service—to do the right thing at the right time. But how do we know what is always the right thing to do? Sometimes many voices are clamoring for our service, from family, church, community, work, and elsewhere. What are we to do then?

At such times, we need to drill up, as the saying goes, and look at our life through God's telescope. In that telescope, the first tube is God himself. We are created for his pleasure, to know, love, and serve him first of all.

The second tube is our spouse, if we are married, followed by our family. If we are married, our first priority after God is to care for our spouse, to help them get to heaven, to meet their needs as best we can on this earth. That means we need to give them our time, our presence, and our attention. There are no substitutes for these three gifts of our self to our spouses.

Our next priority is our family—our children, grandchildren, and loved ones. These especially need our love, at every stage of their lives.

After that comes our work, for indeed, work is part of our vocation to love our spouses and families. We are called to labor with faith, integrity, and excellence. In fact, Paul writes, "Whatever you do, work at it with all your heart, as working for the Lord, not for human masters" (Colossians 3:23).

Finally, then, comes our ministry, our service to the church or broader community. If you follow this telescope, you will see clearly to do well and keep your eyes on the prize!

Above all, love each other deeply,
because love covers over a multitude of sins.

–1 Peter 4:8

The Beatitudes

Blessed are the poor in spirit, for theirs is the kingdom of heaven.

Blessed are those who mourn, for they will be comforted.

Blessed are the meek, for they will inherit the earth.

Blessed are those who hunger and thirst for righteousness, for they will be filled.

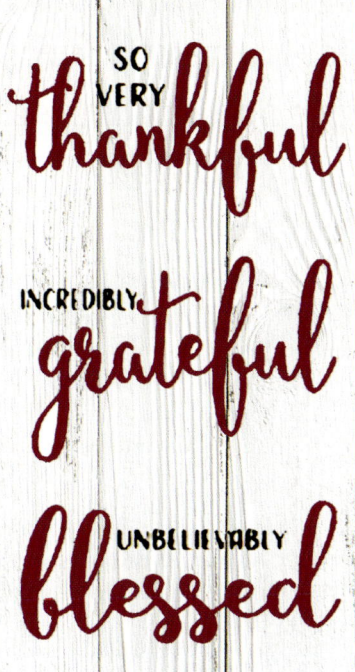

Blessed are the merciful, for they will be shown mercy.

Blessed are the pure in heart, for they will see God.

Blessed are the peacemakers, for they will be called children of God.

Blessed are those who are persecuted because of righteousness, for theirs is the kingdom of heaven.

–Matthew 5:3-12

Servants of Mercy
Florence Nightingale
(1820-1910)
The Founder of Modern Nursing

Florence Nightingale's wealthy British parents baptized her as an Anglican in Florence, Italy, naming her after the city of her birth. Florence learned several European languages and could read the New Testament in its original Greek. Reading the Bible and noted Christian writers like John Wesley, the Puritans, French Dominicans, John Milton, and biographies of missionaries like David Livingstone nourished Florence's faith.

Florence admired people who saw a need, felt a call, and acted upon it. She believed God wanted this of everyone, helping make the world a better place. In the Crimean War, Florence served in the first field hospital ever run by women, working through the night tending the sick and wounded, carrying a lamp to give light for working. She established a hospital just a few miles from the front. There would be greater danger there, but injured men could get quicker attention. She carried out her duties with such efficiency that the army hospital death rate decreased 40% in the first four months. Florence Nightingale soon became known as "The Lady With The Lamp."

Don Howard—A "Regular Guy"

Don Howard grew up in a family whose focus was on helping others and living out their faith. His father, who owned several grocery stores, fed hungry people from his stores, and gave jobs to illiterate people who needed work. He helped them learn to write and taught them how to work and take care of themselves.

Don's grandfather and father also helped people with home repairs. Through their example, Don learned a living faith, taking to heart Jesus' example of feeding the hungry, and his command to Peter, "Feed my sheep." "It shows them someone cares about them," Don reflected.

Don retired early and moved to Arizona to help care for his mother full-time, including taking CNA classes so he could tend to her medical needs so she could remain in her own home. Don also began serving at a local food bank. Many elderly people lived in the community, so Don helped doing home repairs for widows and seniors who couldn't do the work themselves.

"I'm thankful for all I've received and that I can do what Jesus asks us to do," says Don. "It's simply the right thing to do." Don Howard serves with a heart like Jesus.

Merciful Like the Father

In the Old Testament, the words "patient and merciful" are often used to describe the nature of God. He prefers to act in this way with us. The Psalms especially portray for us a God whose mercy is not abstract, but real, as shown in actions which reveal the deep compassion of our Father.

Thus, with our eyes fixed on Jesus, we encounter the love and mercy of God the Father, Son, and Holy Spirit. Jesus reveals the Father to us, and as the apostle John tells us, "God is love" (1 John 4:16). The signs that Jesus worked, especially in favor of sinners, the poor, the marginalized, the sick, and the afflicted, can all teach us mercy and the gift of service.

Jesus reveals a God who will not give up until he has found the lost sheep, forgiven him, and poured into his wounds the abundant oil of compassion and mercy. We are loved! Jesus then calls us to show mercy because mercy has first been shown to us. We are to give mercy, to show mercy, to be merciful ourselves. By its very nature, mercy demands that we do something, that we act.

Jesus, the Heart of a Servant

If you would know the measure of your love for God, just observe your love for your fellowman. Our compassion for others is an accurate gauge of our devotion to God.

–Billy Graham

Jesus Christ is the face of the Father. Jesus said to the apostle Philip, "Whoever has seen me has seen the Father" (John 14:9). Jesus, by His very self—His words, deeds, and being—reveals mercy, the mercy of God. Stop and reflect on that for a moment. Have you looked into Jesus' eyes? Have you felt the Father gazing on you with compassion? It is an important question because that experience is one that can touch your very soul; it is an encounter with a Person who has the power to liberate you from evil, from the bondage of sin, and yes, even from yourself.

As you seek to serve from your heart, know that Jesus wants to love through your heart. He wants to change you more and more into His own image. And that means he wants to serve through you. It is true that when you feed the hungry, clothe the naked, and welcome the stranger, you are doing it to him. However, it is also true that he is serving these little ones through *you*, and thus He is touching you, energizing you, and encouraging you, with *his* servant heart. And that's very good news!

Final Word

"The quality of mercy is not strain'd,
It droppeth as the gentle rain from heaven
Upon the place beneath: it is twice blest;
It blesseth him that gives and him that takes."
–William Shakespeare, *The Merchant of Venice*

True mercy, as evinced in the above quote from *The Merchant of Venice*, is offered in humility and grace, with a certain heartfelt generosity, a spontaneity of spirit. Truly, the quality of mercy is not strained.

You may not be a builder like Don Howard, or a nurse like Florence Nightingale, but you do have gifts God has placed in you to live out his love. The example of Jesus' passionate, overflowing love through simple acts of kindness can inspire each of us to serve. Our gifts of time, talent, and treasure not only bless those we help, but lay a strong foundation for our children and grandchildren, passing a legacy of compassionate loving and giving down through generations.

God calls us to share his mercy with all we meet, to seek to be Christ to the world he died to save and for whom he ever lives to make intercession. May it be so. May you come to know and live the gift of mercy, and to serve with a heart like Jesus. God love you! Amen.